Broke and Going to Mars

USA – Future police state or social state

by

Allen Newman

DORRANCE
PUBLISHING CO
EST. 1920
PITTSBURGH, PENNSYLVANIA 15238

Dorrance Publishing Co
585 Alpha Drive
Pittsburgh, PA 15238
Visit our website at *www.dorrancebookstore.com*

ISBN: 978-1-4809-9164-4
eISBN: 978-1-4809-9378-5

Why did GM go bankrupt? Because they could.
Why did Greece go bankrupt? Because they could.
Why will America go bankrupt? Because they can.

Contents

Foreword

On their journey into bankruptcy, GM had many opportunities to pay down its debt, but at each opportunity, GM executives chose not to do so. In the eighties when GM started its journey into bankruptcy, the first few billions of debt was of no worry to the money lenders; GM had plenty of assets to cover a few billion. During the nineties, a decade of economic prosperity, GM debt continued to increase up past ten billion. Still, the money lenders continued to loan GM money. GM had plenty of assets to cover ten billion, twelve billion, even fourteen billion so the money lenders were not worried. GM was the biggest car company with the best credit rating; people had confidence in getting their money back. At thirteen billion, did Wagner, GMs' CEO, act irresponsibly by continuing to borrow money instead of reducing operational expenses? At thirteen trillion, did President Obama and congress act irresponsibly by continuing to borrow money instead of reducing spending and or raising revenue?

During the presentations to investors, GM continued with the same old lines; they just needed a few good years of car sales and they could take care of the debt and reduce its obligations (billions owed) to the employees' retirement funds. The money lenders continued to loan GM billions. At some twenty billion and the failing economy of 2008, GM went into bankruptcy. According to Alan Greenspan, the financial crash of 2007 was an unforeseen event.

In his book *Overhaul*, Steven Rattner, Obama's car czar, and overseer of GM stated in his first meetings with the GM executives that they did not believe they were in a state of bankruptcy. Instead, they came with their usual presentation to convince the car czar all they needed was a few more billions to tide them through the economic downturn, the same presentation they had used for twenty-some years and twenty-some billions in loans. The U.S. is on a similar path. For the last sixteen years, the federal government has been running a trillion-plus-dollar annual deficit. At twenty trillion in debt and overspending by one trillion annually, our leaders should be worried about financial ruin. Instead, they talk of tax reform and tax reductions to "stimulate" the economy which Regan and George W. Bush both proved will not happen, all the while, funding a needless, expensive trip to Mars. Why did GM go bankrupt? Because they could. Why will America go bankrupt? Because it can.

The default-high debt is exposing a fault in the American Democracy, the inability of politicians to rise above party loyalties; the party is number one, the country number two. Our politicians like the GM executives are in a state of denial and that mindset must be changed. The voters must change that mindset. To do that, the voters need to be educated to the issue and the repercussions of a default. For that to happen, news people, talk show hosts, and debate hosts must move the debt issue front and center. A default will bring us face to face with the question of whether we become a police state or a social state. It is a question I believe the American voter should decide, not Washington bureaucrats.

Chapter 1

Default—the impact

In 452 AD, the great Roman Empire came to an end. The impact on the world was less than a ripple from a pebble tossed into a pond; hardly anyone noticed.

In 1588, Spain went broke and lost its status as an empire. A few years before 1588, King Phillip of Spain decided to teach the English a lesson for their lack of respect and decorum on the high seas. He borrowed large sums of money from the Vatican and money lenders of Europe to build the Spanish Armada. In 1588, it set sail for England. Unfortunately, Spain must have fallen out of favor with the Judeo-Christen god, perhaps due to its harsh and murderous treatment of the native peoples in the distant lands of its empire, for a great storm rose up to scatter and smash the great feet on the shores of its intended conquest. King Phillip would not be able to recoup the cost of the armada from a conquered England to repay the money lenders, so Spain had to withdraw from the world's empire stage as a broke nation. The impact on the world was less than a ripple from a pebble tossed into a pond.

England was next to occupy the world's empire stage and there to remain for some two hundred and fifty years. At one time, it held sway over one fifth of the world as the British were fond of pointing out. The English built and maintained the worlds' largest navy to police its empire. During the 1800s, it was in a constant series of wars from China to Russia to keep it all together. The signal for the end of her empire came with WWI, though it seems the

British missed it. WWII left no doubt, by war's end, through a victor nation, it was broke. It could no longer maintain a large navy and military to hold together an empire; in 1947, the great British Empire came to an end. The impact on the world was that of a ripple from a pebble tossed into a pond; hardy anyone noticed.

America, king of the victor nations, was about to take its turn at running an empire. Almost immediately, the American Empire, the Empire of Good and Plenty, was created, a loose coalition of nations that were bribed (we it call foreign aid or military aid) to be compliant and abide by the wishes of America. In political parlance, it is called hegemony, to hold sway or to dominate others. The basis of the empire was created in the Truman Doctrine and the Marshall Plan in 1947 and the NATO treaty in 1948 to contain and confront the USSR and the spread of communism through economic aid, military aid, and defense treaties. The Truman Doctrine and the Marshall Plan simply morphed into a legacy strategy of foreign aid programs that exist today.

The American Empire was built not to gain wealth from its member nations as all previous empires, but to block the spread of communism and to thwart the USSR from gaining hegemony over those nations. With the collapse of the USSR in the late eighties, it would seem the need to maintain American hegemony over our collection of nations would have ceased, but the bureaucrats and generals whose jobs were at stake ushered forth new reasons to maintain the Empire of Good and Plenty and so it was continued.

Unfortunately, it requires a lot of money to maintain an empire that gives its wealth to its member nations and provides military protection. In all, the U.S. spends over one trillion dollars annually to maintain its Empire of Good and Plenty to maintain hegemony over the world, to maintain the world order as the U.S. wishes it to be. This was all okay with the booming high wage-based economy of the fifties, sixties, and seventies, but now with today's low pay-based economy, it is driving America into financial ruin. When America goes broke (bankrupt), the impact on the world will be that of a one thousand pound meteorite striking our little pond. Instead of a little ripple, the water will be blasted and vaporized out of the pond and where there was a little pond, just a bigger hole will remain, and the world will take notice.

Why the difference? All previous empires looted, pillaged, and took what they could from their subject nations/regions. They also tended to murder, rape, and torture the inhabitants to gain control and to maintain compliant behavior of the native people. When these empires failed or came to an end, the subject nations benefited economically and the inhabitants were happy to see them go.

The American Empire is just the opposite; instead of taking wealth, we give wealth to our puppet (member) nations. To be a member of the American Empire, a nation just has to take our money and military equipment offerings and then act in a manner pleasing to the emperor. The bribe money is called foreign aid and the military equipment is called military aid. As long as the puppet nation acts in a manner the emperor-president desires, they receive their annual stipend. This is not a new tactic; the Roman Empire did the same with Attila to gain his compliant behavior, but it only worked for a while; he eventually attacked the empire anyway. For some, it is not easy to be complaint all the time; the human ego wells up and demands independent action, to be free to choose ones' own course. So it was with General al Sisi of Egypt when in 2017 he was caught trying to purchase several thousand RPGs from North Korea, an enemy of the empire. As Ricky Ricardo would say, "he had some 'splaining to do" as well as a fair amount of groveling to receive his stipend of one hundred million which had been put on hold.

Countries like Egypt, Jordan, Iraq, and Pakistan all have a free military thanks to the American worker/taxpayer. You might think they would at least send us a thank you card. America also funds most of the EU nations' military, the NATO force. Germany and France are not going broke funding the NATO force, but America is. The American worker/tax payer is paying for most of the worlds' military. I ask you, just how much blood can one get from a turnip?

Unfortunately, the great economies of the fifties, sixties, and seventies that created the wealth to create, grow, and maintain the empire has faded away. The continued decline of factories with their good paying jobs, a new low-wage-based economy, never ending wars in the Middle East, tax cuts, maintaining the world's largest military, a great recession, and continuing war on jobs have brought the day of reckoning near. Like the GM executives, our president and legislatures say they just need a few good years of economic growth in order to start paying down the debt. The meteor is about to fall on our little world pond.

When America goes into default, annual spending will have to be reduced by a trillion or more. Not only will America be greatly affected, many nations around the world will be adversely affected. Like Britain and Spain before it to save their countries, America to save itself will have to end its empire, the Empire of Good and Plenty.

Western Europe and the EU will be greatly affected, as they will have to fund their own military (the NATO force). Current U.S. funding, 3.5 percent of GDP of twenty trillion is about 700 billion; a broke America will no longer be able to fund its own and other nations' militaries. With less influence from America, they (the EU) will be free to develop its own European personality. Funding the present NATO force and its operations around the world may be too much of a burden for the EU nations. I would expect some sort of pull back and perhaps reduction of force size. Perhaps Chancellor Merkel and President Macron might wish to send Mr. Putin a Valentine's Day card with a little message like "been thinking of you lately what say we get together and talk". They can choose to embrace the Russian bear as a friend, a new protector or poke and prod it as an enemy like the U.S.; the choice is theirs. Ironically, Russia, because it is not a member of the American Empire, could well benefit from an American default, much to the dismay I suspect of many of our generals.

Other nations of the world that depend on America for free tanks, airplanes, and such like Jordan, Iraq, Pakistan, Egypt, and Afghanistan will have to buy their own tanks, airplanes, and bullets. Japan and South Korea will have to fund their own military which includes staffing their military with their own citizens. These countries will have to raise taxes significantly or find new protectors or seek new alliances.

The UN will also be greatly affected. U.S. operational funds will or should be greatly reduced, resulting in substantial reduction of operational staff and programs. Funding for UN programs like housing and feeding of refugees will be reduced or suspended for a period of time. Recently, Trump suspended a $400 million payment to the Food Aid program. The UN tried to make up for the lost funding, but only obtained pledges for just over half the amount. Currently, the UN cares for about five million refugees. Many will go hungry or perhaps die if other nations do not replace the lost U.S. funds. However, that's the way it will be; the American tax payer can no longer support the world as it is right now. The rest of the world will have to take care of itself while America saves itself from financial ruin. Our politicians will be faced with taking care of its own citizens or taking care of citizens of other countries.

The Middle East region will perhaps be the most affected as the bribe money (foreign aid) will cease to flow. Middle East nations like Jordan, Iraq, Egypt, Afghanistan, and even Israel that depend on foreign aid for their economic stability will fail or fall into economic crisis. Many of these countries that also depend on America for their military will have to buy their own, find another protector or go without. A broke America will no longer be able to fund other nations' militaries. In 1947, the British ended their empire and protector of this region, America, stepped in, and now, America will be stepping out.

Hey, did anyone notice the shiny new billion-dollar NATO headquarters building during President Trump's visit? Mostly paid for by U.S. tax payers. Did anyone receive a thank you card and not share it with me?

Legacy doctrines, policies, and strategies of the forties and fifties to contain and confront the USSR will have to be discontinued. These legacy policies and strategies to contain the USSR and prevent the spread of communism morphed into reasons to maintain the American Empire. Strategies like forward force projection, the triad of deterrence, and maintaining military forces and bases around the world will have to be ended. South Korea will have to fend for itself, build up its own military and pay for its own military or find another protector—the same for Japan and other Asian countries. Many mutual defense treaties would need to be revoked or reworded to release America from military defensive obligations. Certain domestic legacy programs like Space Exploration will have to end. When America officially goes broke (bankrupt), going to Mars will probably no longer seem like a rational thing to do.

The domestic impact on any country that goes broke is significant; the same will be true for America. Greece, Spain, and other European nations that went broke only had to deal with social issues; they did not have to choose between military and social needs. America will be faced with defunding a very large military and its associated security apparatus against funding for social and domestic programs. Voters will be forced to choose whether America becomes a social state like many nations of the world or a police state like a few countries of the world. One thing for sure, the Empire of Good and Plenty will be gone.

All fifty state governors should be concerned, as they will be hit with a triple economic threat. One, many if not all federal grants to the states would be reduced or eliminated. Grants for K through twelve educational systems, medical care, road repair, and first responders would likely be reduced or suspended. Two, revenue sharing will certainly be reduced or suspended. Three, a reduced economy, as many state employee pension funds own U.S. debt; retirees like the Greece retirees will likely take a "hair cut" which means less money for their local economies.

Many states are already running in deficit mode; loss of federal grant and revenue sharing monies would cause these states to make deep cuts and raise taxes. State services will likely be curtailed and many jobs will be cut, increasing a downward economic spiral.

State governors should raise concerns over America's debt load and the negative impact default will have on their states, but all are mum. Why is that? Are they all ignorant of our twenty trillion-dollar debt? Do they not know it is in default territory? Or are they all scared to say so lest it causes some sort of financial panic and then disaster. Not one republican governor, not one democratic governor has said a thing. It is as if they too are part of some seditious 'commy' conspiracy to ruin America. America is not too big to fail, but it is too big to bail out!

Chapter 2

Legacy programs, policies, and strategies

1947 was a momentous year for the modern world, perhaps as momentous as the birth of Christ. It was the year America would forgo George Washington's warning to avoid European entanglements and jump head first into European doings. It was the year Great Britain threw in the empirical towel on their empire and the American Empire of Good and Plenty was born. It was the year American policy, doctrine, and strategy to contain and confront Stalin and the USSR militarily and prevent spread of the communist ideology through economic aid (foreign aid) would define America's actions around the world for next seventy years and still counting. It was the year European nations shelved over two thousand years of nationalism, regional entanglements, and shifting alliances to subordinate themselves to a foreign power on another continent three thousand miles away—America.

The Truman Doctrine was initially to fill a 'protector' role for Turkey and Greece after Britain gave up her empire, leaving Turkey and Greece exposed and vulnerable to USSR aggression. The doctrine soon morphed into a long-term strategy to confront the USSR militarily anywhere in the world.

The Marshall Plan came about in the spring of '47, when statesmen and top generals feared Western Europe which was in dire economic straits would collapse. Their greater fear, however, was these collapsed nations would become easy 'pickin's' for the communist ideology and subsequent soviet domination. If this happened, General George Marshall, now Head of State, and others felt the whole war effort would have been for naught. So an economic plan and strategy for implantation was created. Nations could receive monetary aid if they vowed to reject the communist ideology and soviet interventions and remove certain trade barriers between themselves. The small part of the Marshall Plan was the reconstruction of Western Europe, the part most people learn about in school. The larger part was the open ended strategy of foreign aid and military aid to any nation worldwide to side with America and reject what she rejects and is still with us today.

The final legacy piece is NATO. NATO came about mostly to protect our economic (Marshall Plan) investments in Western Europe. NATO is actually a master stroke of genius. With a stroke of a pen, the nations of Europe set aside thousands of years of autonomy to wage war on one another in favor of a common force funded by all. What a way to prevent future wars amongst those nations while securing our investment, then sell it as a force to confront the USSR. As most European nations were broke, the U.S. picked up the lion's share of funding this new military force. In recent years, it too has expanded its charter and its purpose.

These legacy policies, plans, and doctrines that are the basis for the American Empire are costing America over one trillion dollars a year.

The strategy to deter a nuclear war with the USSR through the triad of nuclear deterrence, a strategy that would ensure America would be able to respond to a first strike by the USSR by land, sea and or air, is still fully funded.

The forward force projection strategy via supersized air craft carriers provides the ability to deliver military force around the world against any country at any time. I presume the reason for the continuance of this strategy is world hubris, although it is sold as a tool to spread freedom and to defend freedom around the world.

One of the great domestic legacy programs is the Interstate Highway System. Prior to the interstate, roads were often built with federal funds via make-work projects during times of economic recessions. Once built, the roads were turned over to the states for upkeep and repair. Not so with the interstate, it has remained the property of the federal government; it has to fund the upkeep and repair of this massive piece of infrastructure.

Space Exploration born out of the Space Race is another legacy program. The high wage-based economy of the sixties and seventies could support this program along with all the other things being funded back then, but not anymore.

The granddaddy of legacy programs, I suppose, is Social Security, enacted during the Great Depression. Medicare, enacted in the sixties, is second of the two big legacy social programs. These two social programs have been at odds with the two empire-creating strategies, the Truman Doctrine and the Marshall Plan, since 2001, competing for funds as America's new low-wage-based economy can no longer support both.

Added to these legacy programs and strategies are the newer, big government agencies, EPA, OHSA, DEA, and the biggest by far, the all-intrusive and top secret DHS. It's all too much; we are going broke.

Chapter 3

Remembering the sixties

The sixties may be the greatest decade in American history. It was a decade in which America did everything and paid for it as we went. It was the decade of the great economy that funded all the things America did. Sometimes, I think today's politicians and policy makers have fond memories of that decade as they continue to fund many of the legacy policies, strategies, and programs from that time period.

Unfortunately, that great economy based on thousands of factories is gone. Instead of paying as we went in the sixties, we now borrow as we go. The nineties, a decade of prosperity, was a haranguer of things to come. We started with around 300 billion of debt and ended the decade with over one trillion of debt. Even with what was considered a good economy, America could no longer sustain its legacy programs, strategies, and policies.

In the fifties and sixties, one could say Americans lived by the motto "we use it we make it, we make it we use it", but by the end of the nineties, it was no longer true; what we used we imported and so it remains today. Trump and the republicans think that lowering corporate taxes will bring back the factories, but taxes have little or nothing to do with that; it is more a matter of customs laws and trade treaties, those same two things that allowed the factories to leave in the first place.

All institutions and enterprises that seek longevity must honor the solvency formula 'E less than or equal R'. Expenses (E) must be less than or equal to revenue (R). GM executives chose to insult the formula to the point of financial default and now our politicians and policy makers are doing the same thing. There is a finite period of time which even America can sustain a trillion-dollar annual deficit.

So what happened to that great sixties economy? First, it went south, then it went west, way west, and now it is just disappearing.

Back in the fifties and sixties, America had tens of thousands of micro economies; each factory was, in effect, the heart of a micro economy. Thousands of towns and small cities owed their economy to a factory or two or several factories for small cities. Tens of thousands of small town main street businesses existed because of their factories. These thousands of micro economies helped to make up that great booming macro economy of the sixties. Any well-learned economist would know that eliminating these thousands of micro economies would adversely affect the macro economy, but in 1964 or so, that is what congress did. Anybody remember any economists making a stink about it?

In 1964, congress ended a collection of laws known as the Bacero laws which allowed Mexicans to enter the country as seasonal farm workers. Mexico, in response to this, instituted an initiative to open factories in the North known as maquiladoras (foreign owned factories) to compensate the region for loss of income, as that is where most of the seasonal workers lived. Congress, at some point, changed our custom laws to allow for production from these factories to enter the U.S. duty free. It's not clear to me if congress acted in concert with Mexico or they were just separate, unrelated actions, but the results were extremely detrimental to America and the American factory worker, but beneficial to Mexico and its workers. What I do not understand is why none of our well-educated economists who advise congress on economic matters have never criticized congress for this action.

China became the next stop for U.S. corporations in the nineties and 2000s. They make almost everything now. Does Wal-Mart or Home Depot sell anything not made in China?

Now it is the robots. Factories exist, but there are no workers in them. I ask you, what good are they? They have no value to a main street business. A robot is not going to mosey into a store and buy something. A workerless factory will provide some local tax revenue, but the local politicians must not be too greedy, lest some bean counter decides it's too much of a burden and recommends moving the factory elsewhere. A few factories may come back, but so what; they will have only a few workers and those will be poorly paid. These factories will not be the heart of a micro economy; in reality, those tens of thousands of micro economies are never coming back.

The next good paying jobs on the chopping block were those that government regulations help to create through limiting competition—specifically, the trucking industry, airlines, and the bus industry. Who remembers the slogan "take the bus and leave the driving to us"? Grey Hound bus drivers used to make a good wage.

Anyone growing up in the sixties would have heard of the Teamsters union, one of the two big unions of the time, the other being the UAW. These two unions were responsible for millions of good paying jobs. However, once congress bought into the old Republican line "competition is good", congress deregulated these industries and let raw capitalism have its day. Today, there are stories of Port Authority truck drivers making less than ten dollars for a sixty-hour work week. Anybody in congress dismayed about this? If Jimmy Hoffa was still alive, some trucking company executive would likely be looking up from a six-foot hole in the ground for perpetuating this outrage. I ask you, what good is a ten-dollar-a-week wage to any level of government? It sure is not going to help pay for a new supersized aircraft carrier.

Airline pilots in the sixties and seventies were at the top of the heap with what I then considered astronomical salaries; for me, the pilots had attained near god-like status. Today, regional airline pilots work two jobs to make ends meet. Long haul pilots retire with little or no retirement funds. That great booming economy of the sixties, it seems, was based on government regulations, strong unions, and limited competition—all things congress destroyed or eliminated in the sixties and seventies. The result is an economy based on low wages where workers struggle to make ends meet while carrying the burden of funding an oversized government. The sooner congressmen and political pundits recognize and acknowledge that the legacy economy of the sixties will not be coming back, the sooner we can start the process to save America from default.

Chapter 4

All the piggy banks have been broken

My source of the following information is primarily from three web sites as follows: mygovcost.org, Wikipedia and thebalance.com. All three were listed by google in response to 'who owns us debt'.

As I recall, at one time, China held a big portion of the U.S. debt back in the nineties or so, but not anymore. They now hold less than 10 percent; Americans themselves now hold a sizable portion in one form or another. On the way to a twenty trillion-dollar debt, politicians smashed and looted several government piggy banks to buy over five trillion of the U.S. debt. To get the details, just do a Google search on "who owns the U.S. debt". Several sites will be listed and they tend to agree on the details. One of the sites divided the debt between two categories: intra government and debt by public, such as private pension funds, mutual funds and national governments. The intra government category, which holds 5.5 trillion of debt, includes the piggy banks of Social Security, Office of Personnel Management, Military Retirement Fund, Medicare and some 200 smaller piggy banks. I wonder how many veterans know they own a piece of the U.S. debt?

The other 14.5 trillion is in the debt by public category. About half of this amount is held by foreign governments (seven billion) and the other half is held by the U.S. Institutions see the following for breakdown:

- The fed – 2.4 trillion
- Mutual funds – 1.6 trillion
- State and local governments (pension funds) – 905 billion
- Banks – 660 billion
- Insurance companies - 340 billion
- All others – 1.6 trillion

In effect, about half, ten trillion, is held by U.S. citizens, mostly through mutual funds, their retirement, and pension funds. So just like Greece, the retired and future retirees will be hit hardest if the U.S. slides into default. They will receive the proverbial "financial hair cut". Retired and soon to retire teachers should be concerned; they own some of that debt just like many state, city, and local government employees. Retired and future retirees need to make this an election issue if they wish the "golden years" retirement dream to continue and be there for them.

So when did the looting of the piggy banks take place? Were people alerted, but no one paid attention? Did congress pull off several midnight heists? Should we alert the FBI? Did it happen under Bush and the republicans or under Obama and the democrats or both? Do they (congress) have a plan to put it all back? Are there any congressmen or senators concerned about the looted piggy banks? If there is, I have yet to hear one to speak of it—certainly not since Donald Trump and the republicans came to town. "Tax cuts" is what I hear—tax cuts to stimulate the new low-wage economy, too entice corporations, to bring back their workerless factories. What we need are tax increases to raise money to restore the piggy banks. People should be concerned; they need to raise the issue with slogans like "restore the piggy banks" or "restore the golden years promise" and others which a politician can latch onto.

The fed owns 2.6 trillion of U.S. debt. What a joke! The government owns its own debt.

George W. Bush famously noted he looked in the Social Security vault and found an IOU from DOD to SS. Does anyone really think the military will pay back its debt to Social Security?

It is understandable that the folks at OMB do not raise issues with a president's budget, as it is part of the White House, but the people at the GAO should at least be getting a little nervous over the twenty trillion-dollar pile of debt. The very least they can do is issue their high water mark projection.

Chapter 5

Saving America—who, what, and how

Politicians like to use election slogans that harken back to better days: "make America great again", and "restore the dream". What we need are politicians that use the word 'save' in their slogans like "save America from financial ruin" or "save America from bankruptcy" or "save the American Dream".

For several years prior to the 2016 elections, Paul Ryan and the republicans railed against the trillion-dollar annual deficit and mile-high debt and put forth that if elected, they would demonstrate physical responsibility. However, Paul Ryan reneged on his rhetoric, as did all the other republicans. Instead of putting his country first, Paul put loyalty to the party's leader first. The White House staged an event with Trump and the republicans congratulating each other in front of the Capital. If this event had happened 2400 years ago in Rome, Gibbon might have described the scene "as bending before the purple".

Who will step forward and make "saving American from bankruptcy" an election motto? Which of the two major parties will ignore its past political mottos and platforms to proclaim a bleak future if the current course of things do not change? Which one will champion a new motto "save America" or "save the American Dream"? One thing I am certain of, politicians will not by themselves proclaim the need to "save" America. They will have to be led, pushed to embrace that idea, that concept, and that's the job of the American voter.

Selling the idea to voters that America needs to be saved will take some time and effort, as most probably are not aware of the looted piggy banks and pending disaster. Cutting spending by a trillion dollars will, after all, have a significant, adverse impact on the way things are. First and foremost is the economy, which will go into recession for some period of time. One to two million government employees will have to be dismissed. Big government and BIG military will have to shrink. Orders for new ships, airplanes, tanks, and such will have to be cancelled or put on hold, causing more people to lose their jobs. Certain noncritical departments and agencies will have to endure significant cuts like NASA, DEA, OSHA, and such. Maybe the trip to Mars will not seem so important at his point.

State governments will face a loss of government grants and revenue sharing. Educational institutions will also face financial cuts. The Japanese Emperor Hirohito told his people at the end of WWII as the U.S. occupation was about to begin, "We must bear the unbearable... we must endure the unendurable." So it must be for Americans to bear economic suffering and loss of world hegemony to atone for the financial sins of the past. Can all this be avoided? Sure, but congress would have to reduce BIG military and let the empire go, raise taxes, and start restoring the looted piggy banks, but the history of congress is they cannot do this without the consent of the voters. As long as the voters are ignorant of the situation, they will of course not force the issue.

We must first acknowledge the fact that we are nearing the end of the rope at twenty trillion of debt. I speculate that default will occur somewhere between twenty and twenty-five trillion of debt. As noted earlier, all the piggy banks have all been looted; China seems more interested in spending its money on building economic pathways to other parts of the world than buying U.S. debt. Special arrangements with Saudi Arabia have induced them to acquire over two trillion of our debt, but they may be nearing the end of their tolerance for holding U.S. debt. I guess that leaves the Rothschilds to pick up the tab. The point is, the U.S. is running out of money pots to raid and countries that are willing to buy U.S. debt.

This past September, Toys R Us went into bankruptcy; the event was unexpected and took business analysis by surprise. That's how it happens. A holder of bonds that had matured wanted their money instead of just rolling it over again; Toys R Us did not have the money to pay the bond holder and so had to declare bankruptcy. The event was unforeseen and unpredictable—much the same thing Mr. Greenspan told congress of the 2008 financial crash.

Talk show hosts must start talking about it. CNN, FOX, PBS, and CNBC must all raise awareness to the pending disaster—no sugar coating it. ABC, CBS, and NBC need to address the issue on their nightly news programs. The issue should be addressed from various social standpoints. Internet bloggers and sites like Brightbart, Politico, and such need to address the issue. Everybody needs to bring the issue front and center above all others. Political programs like *Meet the Press* and *Washington Week* need to raise the specter of default with their guests.

A standard set of questions must be asked over and over to guests. What trillion-dollar mark do they think will cause default? Are they willing to give up the Empire of Good and Plenty to save America? Would they give up funding NATO to save America? Are they willing to reduce BIG military by 70-80 percent to what is just needed for defense for x period of time to prevent default? Would they cut all foreign aid and spending before cutting domestic spending? In order to balance the budget (honor the solvency formula), what specific actions do they (would they) advocate for? Would they place a temporary tax on imports and or corporations to pay down the debt? These questions and a few others like them need to be asked over and over until politicians take up the cause. Which is a more serious threat to America, North Korea or default? Everybody is talking about North Korea, but no one is talking about default. Occasionally, the amount of debt is mentioned, but not the threat of default.

Presidential debate hosts must frame all questions in context of financial default if legacy policies, strategies, and programs continue to be promoted. That is, if we are going bankrupt, how can we continue to afford to do that which a candidate is proposing? Are candidates aware of the looted piggy banks? Certain standard responses must not go unchallenged such as "our national interests are at stake". What national interest? Is that particular national interest more important than averting default? Debate hosts have to dispel the myth that reduced taxes leads to eventual revenue growth. It did not in the nineties after Reagan's eighties tax cuts, as we ended that decade with our first trillion dollars of debt. It did not after George W. Bush's tax cuts, as we have had a trillion-dollar annual deficit ever since. Debate hosts should pose the question, "if president, what would you advise if we go into default" or "if president, what plan would you put forth to restore the looted piggy banks?" The debate hosts simply must bring financial default front and center in order for it to receive proper attention.

The generals, admirals, and Joint Chiefs of Staff should consider threat of default their greatest threat. Not ISIS, not Russia, not North Korea but financial default. The generals need to get it in their heads what a default would likely entail. The days of BIG military will certainly be over. With default, the generals may be on the outside looking in as congress ponders the fate of America—whether it will become a military state or a social state.

Before it is too late, the generals themselves should set some trillion-dollar debt mark on which to take some action. Perhaps they should have a contingency plan ready that addresses default just in case. The generals should ask questions about their own retirement piggy bank. Has it been smashed and looted? If yes, why did congress do that? The generals can become advocates of financial solvency, they can become advocates of saving the great democracy or they can keep their heads in the sand and let things go kaput.

Just to pay off the debt at say, five hundred billion a year would take forty years. That includes cutting spending and or raising revenue by one and a half trillion annually so not to add more to the debt total. Restoring financial stability will neither be easy nor popular. Everyone will have to give up something.

Governors of all fifty states should be concerned, as they will likely be hit with a double whammy. Whammy one will be the reduction or elimination of revenue sharing and whammy two, a reduction or elimination of block grants for education, first responders, and all other grant monies. This, in turn, will impact all school districts that receive grant money to fund operations and school programs and most do. Most states will not be able to raise taxes sufficiently to replace the lost revenue so cuts will have to be made. Local fire and police units will also suffer a similar fate, as many states will not be able to make up the lost revenue. State governors should stop acting blissful and dumb to their impending future if the U.S. goes into default. They, the states, will be lucky to be second on the list of those the federal bureaucrats will seek to save, as they will be in competition with BIG military and the Empire of Good and Plenty for second place.

Default will likely happen in one of three unpredictable ways. One, the U.S. will miss an interest payment which is a common way institutions go into default. According to Wikipedia, the U.S. technically went into default in 1979 on missing an interest payment due date, but many consider it a "delayed payment", as the payment was eventually made. Two, another common way, a bond holder (T-note) will wish to redeem a mature bond, but the treasury cannot pay back the bond due to a lack of money; this is the manner Toys R Us went into default. Three, one fine day, the Treasury will seek to sell eighty billion dollars or so of bonds at 2 percent or so to cover upcoming monthly bills and payments, but no one will raise their hand. The risk of default is becoming too great for a lousy 2 percent return. At this point, there will be no good options for the Treasury Secretary and America. The secretary will have to withdraw the offering and then discuss with the president and policy makers what to do. Increasing the rate of return to 4 or 5 percent is not sustainable for the U.S., as debt interest payment would rise to one trillion a year. Printing billions of dollars by the fed to buy the offering is inflationary and is but a very short term solution.

Then there is the way Iceland went bankrupt; their banking system collapsed and pulled the country into default. The U.S. could, of course, just declare itself in default and proceed accordingly, whatever that means. Here comes the hair cut.

No more "make America great again" slogans—please.

Chapter 6

Saving America—

giving up legacy programs, policies, strategies, and empire

The space program, born of the space race with the USSR, a darling of the sixties and seventies, but today's low wage based economy and reduced tax revenues can no longer fund it along with all the other things. Is it really necessary to go to Mars? Which is more important, going to Mars or taking care of America and its citizens? We have gotten to a point where decisions of what to keep and what to discard have to be made.

We were once the defender of a defeated and broke Europe. Europe is no longer broke, but we are. Europe needs to pay for its own military. The USSR is gone and Russia is not the big threat the USSR was. Russia has made overtures to join NATO, but NATO bureaucrats rebuked their offers. I suspect NATO policy makers were protecting their jobs more than protecting Europe from a ghost of the past. With no real Russian military threat, NATO does not need to exist; however, to keep their jobs, NATO policy makers must keep the threat alive. Our own leaders must decide between funding NATO (Europe's military) or eliminating something else or raising taxes. We are near default; we cannot do it all anymore. Trump had the right idea; he just did not have the perseverance or know how to carry it through. Perhaps if he had stated "we are going broke… we can no longer fund your military", things might have gone differently.

Maintaining triad of deterrence was another legacy policy of the sixties when the USSR was a threat. The USSR is gone and so is the threat. Russia has made efforts to be friendly, join NATO, etc., but like NATO policy makers, U.S. policy makers, generals, and leaders have rebuked their efforts. I suspect both have rejected Russian advances for the same reasons; without a Russian threat, the reason to maintain BIG military and all those military related jobs goes away.

The big economy of the sixties is gone; we are going broke, but we continue to maintain the triad of deterrence. A news article reported the Trump Administration is funding efforts to update B52 crew's quarters next to the big bomber pads used to station fully loaded and ready to fly B52 bombers in "alert" status. These ready-to-fly bombers were once part of the triad of deterrence. A 1991 treaty with Russia has outlawed these "alert" status bombers so why spend money updating their pads? We are also spending money to update another leg of the deterrence: the nuclear missile submarines, affection ally called "boomers" to replace the existing fleet. Of course, we continue to maintain our underground missiles. The spending just never stops. Congress needs to decide to maintain this policy and give up something else or raise taxes. FDR once thought if the USSR and America could get along after the end of the war, then they, with the new, but not yet created UN could maintain world order. Back then, the U.S. was willing, but not the USSR; now Russia is willing but not America.

We continue to maintain world hegemony that was based on the old, anti-communism strategy. The communist threat is gone, but not the hegemony strategy. After the fall of the USSR, America could have let the world go its own way, but instead, found new reasons to continue PAC Americana. One reason has become maintaining global economic stability—it's good for the countries of the empire and it is good for U.S. corporations. Perhaps the biggest reason is simply satisfying the egos of the bureaucrats and policy makers. Running the world, I imagine, is fairly intoxicating, making decisions that affect nations, determining which nations to embrace, which to exclude from the empire, etc., but it does come with a cost—a cost we can no longer afford; we are going broke.

Defender of the free world was another post-WWII policy. A noble concept and policy, but one the U.S. economy and taxpayer can no longer support.

America's politicians and policy makers need to get it in their heads that this noble burden is more than today's economy can support. The great communist threat is gone; they need to let go of the policy.

Over the course of the last sixty years, our legislatures have allowed the generals too much voice and influence in policy making. Generals do not want wars to end; this is evident in our never-ending wars in Iraq, Afghanistan, and now Syria. Generals should only wag war, they should not make policy; policy is the domain of politicians. In a democracy, politicians start the wars and politicians end the wars; generals fight the wars and up through 2000, that's the way it was. Unfortunately, our politicians have come to fear the generals; what the generals want they now get. If they do not wish to leave Afghanistan, then we will not leave; the politicians refuse to cut funding for their ongoing forever war. A senator from the south was once quoted in a web news article "whatever the generals want they will get". Senators with that frame of mind are no friends of democracy. In a democracy, the military is a tool of the legislature (congress); in a military state like Egypt, congress is a tool of the military. Increasingly it seems since 9/11, our politicians have become tools for the military.

Chapter 7

The Interstate—a modern Appian Way

In the fifties and sixties, when the economy was good and growing, the federal government had plenty of money to build the road system. Initially, it had more to do with defending the country in the event of an attack. The military could move men and material around the country in an expedient manner from east to west, north to south, and vice versa. The continued building of the interstate roadway after meeting military requirements eventually became a political boondoggle. Military planners avoided cities while political planners went right through the middle of them. Local politicians wanted beltways around their cities and the military just wanted to go from one side of the country to the other.

After a few years, local politicians wanted a wider interstate (more lanes) and congress obliged them. I75 north of Atlanta is now six lanes wide in one direction. Is six the limit or is there no limit to this madness?

Boston's 'big dig' project finally convinced the bureaucrats to at least stop any further downtown projects. As well it should, at a cost of over one billion dollars per mile of expressway.

Atlanta is a fine example of expressway overbuild by congress and the bureaucracy—several hundred miles of expressways snaking out from the beltway loop into distant 'burbs' are strictly local use roads built with federal funds. One could argue that it helped to keep the economy going back in the day.

We have over 45,000 miles of expressway in America. Half of that is sufficient to meet military needs—three expressways east to west and five or six north to south, about 15,000 miles.

The point is this: when congress finally cuts spending by one and a half trillion to stop increasing the debt and to start paying it off, funds to maintain this massive piece of infrastructure may well dry up or be significantly reduced. The states may in the end have to maintain their own sections of this massive thing not considered militarily significant. Cities are already erecting toll stations along sections leading in and out of or around their city. In the future, it may become a rich man's road, as employees of the new low-wage economy will not be able to afford the toll rates. Many states are already in debt and maintenance of these roads is expensive. The prospect is fairly good that many sections of this modern day marvel will become much like that marvel of two thousand three hundred years ago, the Appian Way of the Roman Republic.

Chapter 8

Congress, the fed, and the baby boomers

For two hundred years, America has been the land of milk and honey, but if congress does not soon act financially responsible, it will turn to the land of sour milk and lemons of vanishing dreams and lost hope. Millions of Americans' retirement accounts have been looted to pay for years of trillion-dollar deficits and congress apparently has no plans to put it back. If they did, they would have to raise taxes and or cut spending and a republican congress will do neither. The republican president and congress, instead, are working to do just the opposite, cut taxes (revenue) and increase spending by starting a big, new infrastructure project (the wall) and increase military spending; it's still not big enough—nothing about restoring our retirement piggy banks. Ooh republican financial conservatives, where art thou? Why doesn't thou speak?

Some two hundred years ago, the great democratic experiment began. The democracy survived a savage civil war, countless banking and financial crises, a great depression, and a great war, but now is facing its greatest crisis, which left unattended, may well bring about its downfall.

While wars and depressions are hard to ignore, financial insolvency is easy to ignore, as long as no one talks about it and no one is talking about it. The republicans are not talking about it. The democrats are not talking about it. State governors are not talking about it. The generals are not talking about it. The news talk show hosts are not talking about it. The hosts of *Meet the Press* and *Washington Week* are not talking about it. By chance, I did hear Maria Bartiromo of MSNBC mention it once. The nightly news programs of ABC, NBC, CBS, and PBS do not mention it. If no one is talking about it, then for certain, congress is not going to talk about it.

Twenty trillion dollars is a lot to ignore. Even for the U.S., twenty trillion is a lot of money. America can survive a default, but the Empire of Good and Plenty cannot; it will have to go. If congress is to save America from default, it will first need a good prodding.

It took the Brits two years to acknowledge the reality that their empire was at an end. They ended WWII broke, in debt, and with a ruined economy, yet they clung to the remnants of their empire for two years until the spring of 1947, when reality finally set in. They could either let the empire go and save the country or sink with the empire; they let the empire go. It was, I'm sure, a tough decision to make by those born, raised, and schooled as a member of the empire, being told as a youngster in grade school you will become stewards of the empire, its caretakers, and then growing up, partaking in the glory of the empire only to be the ones to decide to let it go. American politicians are still in the denial stage that our debt is not an issue to be concerned about.

The baby boomers are now checking out of the work force and into retirement. Unfortunately, it may be bad timing; with a default-high debt, congress will have to decide whether to continue the Empire of Good and Plenty and renege on the promise of the golden years dream or to let the empire go and keep the promise of the golden years dream. The millions of baby boomers, if they want the promise kept, will have to fight for it. However, first they need to be made aware that they are on the hook for ten trillion of the twenty trillion-dollar debt.

The state governors need to take on this responsibility. They need to educate their citizens to the situation by going on talk shows, making appearances on the nightly news programs, and sending out literature, tweets and Facebook messages—"a call to arms" sort of thing. A great battle of wills, the bureaucrats of the Empire of Good and Plenty versus the baby boomers will have to be waged. Our debt situation will support one or the other, but not both. Those who wish to live the golden years dream will have to drain the swamp by voting out every incumbent and voting in those who will restore the piggy banks (pay down the debt) and let the empire go—America the country first, its citizens second, and everything and everybody else third.

Within ten years (2028), most of the baby boomers will be out of the work force and in retirement, the last leg of their socioeconomic journey. This bulge of humanity has been responsible for impacting the various economic and social institutions all along their journey through life. First, the primary educational systems had to expand to accommodate them—build new facilities, hire more staff, buy more buses, and so on. The retailers that service this new mass also grew—more malls, more stores, more stuff to sell. Then, the higher educational institutions had to expand to accommodate the bulge of eager-to-be-educated boomers. Then, they went into the work force, expanding and sustaining a great economy, buying houses and all the stuff to put in them, buying recreational toys, boats, four wheelers, campers, and camping stuff so to enjoy life with the family and living the American Dream. Now, the final leg of the journey and the final economic segments to receive the boomer bump—the medical care and retirement segments, more hospitals to build, more doctors, nurses, and staff to hire, more medical equipment to buy, more sun cities to build, oh what joy for the CEOs of companies of these economic segments. Unfortunately, the long awaited bump may be little more than a pipe dream, a fantasy for the baby boomer, now turned into a quandary for the dream holders, their congressman. A mountain of debt, an empire to fund, and the golden years promise is too much for a low-wage-based economy to bear; the fight for the golden years dollar is about to begin and in the words of General Robert Neller, it will be a big ass fight.

In addressing 300 marines newly stationed in Norway in 2017, the senior four-star general commandant of the marines and member of the Joint Chiefs of Staff told the marines to be prepared for the big ass battle coming. He, of course, was referring to the big battle with the USSR that never took place. With the collapse of the USSR in 1988, the threat of that battle vanished. So now, the battle is a fantasy battle, as Russia has but a small fraction of that big military the USSR maintained. Also, the U.S. military is much more technically advanced than Russia's military; the big ass battle with them in Europe would be similar to the wars with Iraq, as it would be over in a couple of weeks. General Neller keeps the fantasy battle alive to convince our congressmen to keep funding a BIG military to fight that battle. The baby boomers number in the millions and while there are only four members in the Joint Chiefs of Staff, but they have BIG influence with congress. The generals are just one part of the problem for the boomers; how the future congresses deal with the debt is the big issue.

The fed would, in normal times, have some sway in the fight, but a near-default debt and the new low-wage-based economy may make the fed impendent. With a fiscally responsible congress, the fed could hold sway over the economy and inflation by raising or lowering interest rates. However, with today's irresponsible congress, high debt, and a low-wage-economy congress may well be calling all the shots; the fed may well become a spectator. That is to say, if we enter into another recession, the fed will be powerless to act, as interest rates are already near zero. Congress, with its new tax cuts, wants the economy to heat up to increase tax revenues, but if it does, the fed would normally raise interest rates to cool it down, but that action would increase the risk of default if the planned tax revenues are reduced. The fed may well be in a box. To pay down the debt, congress must cut spending and raise taxes; together, those two actions would likely induce a recession and still remaining is the matter of the empire versus the golden years promise. With the prospect of a long-term recession, one or the other must go.

Of the three, the fed, congress, and baby boomers, the baby boomers should have the most to say about things, but first, they must be made aware of the situation. News programs, talk show hosts, state governors, and internet bloggers need to raise the issue. The boomers next need to vote out everybody who has allowed this situation to come about, no exceptions; all current senators and representatives must go. Vote in only those who will save the social promises made fifty years ago. Vote in only those who promise to restore our piggy banks, all ten trillion. Vote in only those who will forego the Empire of Good and Plenty to save America from default. Most importantly, vote only for a president who will lead the effort and be willing to forego a second term to save the country from financial default and subsequent economic crisis in which massive federal spending cuts will have to be made which most likely will impact many social and welfare programs.

We expect our enemies to employ weapons of mass destruction in their attempt to destroy us; what we do not expect is our own congressmen using our constitution to destroy us, but that is what our democratic and republican congressmen are doing. They use the power granted to them to set the budget and pass laws. With a mountain-high debt created by both parties, the last twelve trillion by the democrats, the current tax cut (revenue cut) law passed by the republicans should be viewed as nothing less than an incompetent and irresponsible act. Instead of raising revenue to pay down the debt to reduce the risk of default, they reduced revenue and increased the risk of default. I ask if America slides into default which causes another financial crisis that could well ruin it, is that any worse than what Benedict Arnold sought to accomplish? Where was the fed chairman during this process? Not one critical comment did he offer to the revenue reduction plan when an increase, a big increase was needed. The fed chairperson could have used the talk show circuit to advance the need to increase revenue, but chose to remain silent. The true America hero to emerge was Savannah Guthrie of NBC, who challenged Paul Ryan for living in a fantasy world.

I say all our incumbent congressional leaders should be treated as incompetent and irresponsible and voted out of office. Chuck Schumer and Nancy Pelosi, of the democrats and Paul Ryan and Mitch McConnell of the republicans. They must all pay for their incompetent, irresponsible behavior. We need leaders who will put their country first and their party second. At some point in time this continued action to ignore default-high debt must be viewed not just as irresponsible, but as treasonous. They must be replaced by people who will act responsibly and raise taxes, who will put America before their party, who will honor the social contracts. If corporations want BIG military, then they should expect to pay BIG taxes. If the politicians and bureaucrats want to run an empire then they should expect to pay for it.

Chapter 9

Immigration

Up through the forties or so, immigrants made do with what they had when they got here. Their first jobs were often for very low wages, long hours, and no benefits. No social programs existed to get them acquainted with America and provide them with food and shelter until they found employment. Nowadays, immigrants receive free medical care, receive food and shelter for some period of time, even free phones and such. With America's default-high debt, perhaps America should call for a moratorium on immigration including refugees. Immigrants went from costing the government almost nothing to millions of dollars.

Immigration is a darling of the left and many a politician. The history of "give us your poor and downtrodden" is ingrained in our brains. However, times have changed; we are broke. Social programs for our own citizens are being cut, but immigrant programs get better and more costly; it's time we look at immigration in light of the new times. We can revert back to the way it was in the 1890s, make do as best one can with no government assistance, or we can put a moratorium on immigration until we fix our debt problem and can maintain funding for desirable social programs for our own citizens.

Corporate CEOs who like cheap labor that new immigrants provide will mount some sort of America, the land of opportunity, the compassionate campaign to keep the inflow coming and make us feel guilty for harboring thoughts of an immigrant moratorium. However, the reality of default-high debt and a new low-wage economy will eventually force unwanted decisions to be made.

Chapter 10

Saving America from default—

a simple strategy—a matter of druthers

In their introduction summary, the authors of *White House Burning* make the following summation; comments in parentheses are my comments:

> If the American people understand where our national debt came from (their smashed piggy banks), the stakes involved (The American Golden Years Retirement Dream) and the tradeoffs in reducing the debt (the Empire of Good and Plenty and BIG military versus a social state like Canada), we will be able to choose the future that we want for our government and our society.

My view on their statement: "hope springs eternal in the human breast".

While I am not a Harvard graduate with a major in economics like Simon Johnson, a well-heeled, well-educated economist, coauthor of *White House Burning* and *13 Bankers*, I am at least well read. According to Mr. Johnson, America, with a twenty trillion-dollar debt, should be in default, but we are not. In their book, *White House Burning*, published in 2012, Johnson and Kwak discuss the importance of a country being able to go into debt to fund wars or stimulate economic growth, but also noted the importance of paying off that debt. By 2018, they projected U.S. debt to be thirteen trillion if George W. Bush's tax cuts were left intact. They only missed the mark by seven trillion. They pound home the point that as long as a country has good credit worthiness, it will not only be able to borrow money, but also borrow it at a low rate of interest, which so far has been the case with America or so it seems. The fed has picked up three trillion of the tab while federal and state government piggy banks have been raided to the tune of several trillion. I suspect if all twenty trillion had come from outside sources, the interest rate would be much higher.

I found their book to be a good read, but it was a bit to clinical, as they did not personalize the debt. The debt is affecting my retirement dream and I am a pre-baby boomer. All future retirees—policemen, fireman, teachers, government employees, and baby boomers—will be adversely affected much more than me. For the most part, Johnson and Kwak only come up to the point of default; they do not dwell on what happens to America, its social programs, its empire, and the world in the event of default, which is my start point.

They also make the point that if Americans understand who owns the debt, they will act (vote) according to their understanding, with which I agree. What the authors failed do is to inform us how the masses are to be educated. How does one educate 120 million voters to the debt situation? I simply suggest we start talking about it. We talk about a threat from North Korea ad nauseam, but nary a word about the threat of default. Unlike Greece, Americans will have to choose between funding an empire and funding its domestic programs. Also, Americans will have to choose between funding a BIG military or funding social and welfare programs. It has to become a personal issue for the voter.

The authors presented a plan to save America from default, again, a bit clinical, I thought, and a bit unrealistic now that America is entering into a low-wage-based economy. They theorized that if some taxes are raised and some spending is reduced, all will be okay; we can still go to Mars and not go broke, and we can keep the empire and the golden years promise and not go broke and that, I believe, is impossible. To be fair, they did not anticipate congress would be irresponsible and allow the debt to climb to twenty trillion dollars. I no longer envision any congress with its current incumbents to act rationally on behalf of America, its citizens, and future retirees. No plan can be acceptable to both parties so why bother with the effort? We simply have to elect a new generation of individuals to congress who understand and are willing to accept the limitations of a low-wage-based economy. America is becoming like Mexico; we need a president and a congress to accept that new reality. A new reality—we need to raise revenue by at least a trillion dollars and reduce spending by a trillion dollars to pay down the debt in some reasonable timeframe. Just as the events of 1947 were a shockwave for America and Europe, so will our financial default be a shockwave to both, as well as too much of the world.

One way out is for the baby boomers and future retirees of America to get selfish, vote out all those who seek to take away their retirement dream, and vote in only those who support their selfish wants, to honor their contract with America and to restore their piggy banks. Is it too much to ask for a retirement future like the French and Germans enjoy? Yet, to do that, people must be made aware of the situation and choices before them.

Can there be another way? Congress could raise taxes on corporations, imports etc. sufficiently to pay down the debt by say one trillion a year (a twenty-year plan), while not adding more to the debt, which would mean more taxes or letting something go. We could even let the CEO of GE decide what to do, raise corporate taxes a bit more or cancel the trip to Mars. However, as we have seen from congress, party loyalty is number one and the country is number two.

At one point, I thought perhaps a simple plan might work such as putting all spending into one of seven priority categories. Category one, the highest priority, would contain spending for national defense and certain critical social programs like SS and Medicare. Categories two through five would contain all the other domestic spending programs. Categories six and seven would be for foreign spending programs. All spending not for king, country, and the citizens would be considered foreign. One caveat, the military budget would be reduced to 20 percent of present funding, as much of the current spending is for the empire.

Whenever spending needed to be reduced, the programs in the lowest priority category would be cut first—no debate except how much and which ones to affect in that category. This has the benefit of greatly reducing debate.

A few other rules could be devised, such as cuts in the next higher level category could not take place until some level of spending reductions had been reach in the next lower level category, say 90 percent or whatever. So if a hundred billion dollars needed to be cut from the budget, items in categories seven and six would be cut or eliminated first, and if more cuts were needed, then items in category five would be affected and so on—simple and relatively painless. Still, every plan has its pros and cons and politicians will be quick to point out the cons even for a simple plan.

The history of congress and presidents is to cut domestic spending, while increasing or maintaining foreign spending. I just happen to feel that America and its citizens should be ranked one and two respectively and everything and everybody else number three, which includes the empire. If cuts are to be made, cut number three items first. Apparently, the only way to ensure that is to devise a plan and strategy that would force cuts in some predetermined manner so to eliminate the usual debate or to vote in a new batch of people committed to honoring America's social contracts with its citizens.

At seven trillion of debt, George W. Bush did not address the debt in his last State of the Union address. At nineteen trillion, Barak Obama did not address the debt in his last State of the Union address. At twenty trillion of debt, Donald Trump did not address the debt in his first State of the Union address. As the saying goes, ignorance is bliss. Will we ever have a president who will address the debt in their State of the Union address before we actually go into default? People—the voters, talk show hosts, bloggers, etc. must force the issue front and center before it is too late.

To balance the budget and start repaying the piggy banks, congress must cut spending and or raise revenue by a trillion and a half or so annually. There is simply no way for them to do that with their current collective state of mind that all is okay. We need new people with a different state of mind, one that is willing to accept the reality of a low-wage-based economy.

America needs another hero like Andrew Jackson—a hero of the times. America needs someone who is willing to reverse course and give up a second term. America needs a person to sell us on hard times, to accept loss of empire and world hubris to save the country, to give up BIG military for just a national defense posture and we must give up the trip to Mars. Only two people come to mind that could pull it off, Elizabeth Warren and Donald Trump. They both have notoriety and good speaking skills. Selling people on hard times may sound like a difficult thing, but Americans love their country, Americans love a good cause, and they love pulling together to accomplish a good cause. All we need is a hero, a champion to lead us in that cause.

www.ingramcontent.com/pod-product-compliance
Lightning Source LLC
Chambersburg PA
CBHW070503290526
45790CB00003B/1074